Institute of Leadership
& Management

superseries

Managing Conflict in the Workplace

FIFTH EDITION

Published for the
Institute of Leadership & Management

ELSEVIER

AMSTERDAM • BOSTON • HEIDELBERG • LONDON • NEW YORK • OXFORD
PARIS • SAN DIEGO • SAN FRANCISCO • SINGAPORE • SYDNEY • TOKYO
Pergamon Flexible Learning is an imprint of Elsevier

Pergamon
Flexible
Learning

Pergamon Flexible Learning is an imprint of Elsevier
Linacre House, Jordan Hill, Oxford OX2 8DP, UK
30 Corporate Drive, Suite 400, Burlington, MA 01803, USA

First edition 1986
Second edition 1991
Third edition 1997
Fourth edition 2003
Fifth edition 2007

Editor: David Pardey

Based on material in previous editions of this work

The views expressed in this work are those of the authors and do
not necessarily reflect those of the Institute of Leadership &
Management or of the publisher

Notice
No responsibility is assumed by the publisher for any injury and/or damage to persons or
property as a matter of products liability, negligence or otherwise, or from any use or operation
of any methods, products, instructions or ideas contained in the material herein

British Library Cataloguing in Publication Data
A catalogue record for this book is available from the British Library

Library of Congress Cataloguing in Publication Data
A catalogue record for this book is available from the Library of Congress

ISBN 978-0-08-046416-9

For information on all Pergamon Flexible Learning publications
visit our website at http://books.elsevier.com

Institute of Leadership & Management
Registered Office
1 Giltspur Street
London
EC1A 9DD
Telephone: 020 7294 2470
www.i-l-m.com
ILM is part of the City & Guilds Group

Typeset by Charon Tec Ltd (A Macmillan Company), Chennai, India
www.charontec.com
Printed and bound in Great Britain

07 08 09 10 11   10 9 8 7 6 5 4 3 2 1

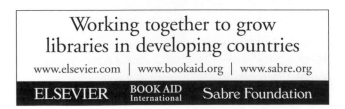

Contents

Series preface

Whether you are a tutor/trainer or studying management development to further your career, Super Series provides an exciting and flexible resource to help you to achieve your goals. The fifth edition is completely new and up-to-date, and has been structured to perfectly match the Institute of Leadership & Management (ILM)'s new unit-based qualifications for first line managers. It also harmonizes with the 2004 national occupational standards in management and leadership, providing an invaluable resource for S/NVQs at Level 3 in Management.

Super Series is equally valuable for anyone tutoring or studying any management programmes at this level, whether leading to a qualification or not. Individual workbooks also support short programmes, which may be recognized by ILM as Endorsed or Development Awards, or provide the ideal way to undertake CPD activities.

For learners, coping with all the pressures of today's world, Super Series offers you the flexibility to study at your own pace to fit around your professional and other commitments. You don't need a PC or to attend classes at a specific time – choose when and where to study to suit yourself! And you will always have the complete workbook as a quick reference just when you need it.

For tutors/trainers, Super Series provides an invaluable guide to what needs to be covered, and in what depth. It also allows learners who miss occasional sessions to 'catch up' by dipping into the series.

Super Series provides unrivalled support for all those involved in first line management and supervision.

Unit specification

Title:	Managing conflict in the workplace	Unit Ref:	M3.14
Level:	3		
Credit value:	1		

Learning outcomes *The learner will*	Assessment criteria *The learner can (in an organization with which the learner is familiar)*	
1. Know how to resolve conflict in the workplace	1.1	Identify causes of conflict at work
	1.2	Describe the stages in the development of conflict
	1.3	Explain the effects of conflict on individual and team performance at work
	1.4	Explain any recognized technique the manager could use to minimize and resolve conflict in the workplace
	1.5	Describe how a manager could create harmony at work and engender a positive atmosphere in order to minimize the adverse effects of conflict

Workbook
introduction

1 ILM Super Series study links

This workbook addresses the issues of managing conflict. Should you wish to extend your study to other Super Series workbooks covering related or different subject areas, you will find a comprehensive list at the back of this book.

2 Links to ILM qualifications

This workbook relates to the learning outcomes of Unit M3.14 Managing conflict in the workplace from the ILM Level 3 Award, Certificate and Diploma in First Line Management.

3 Links to S/NVQs in management

This workbook relates to the following Unit of the Management Standards which are used in S/NVQs in Management, as well as a range of other S/NVQs:

B6. Provide leadership in your area of responsibility

4 Workbook objectives

The purpose of this workbook is to look at conflict in the workplace. You will learn about the causes of conflict and how you can attempt to prevent conflict occurring. It also looks at what you need to do if conflict does occur, to support individuals and deal with its effects.

Session A looks at conflict in the workplace. Nearly all conflicts involve underlying emotional issues. The stronger the feelings, the more difficult the resolution. To resolve conflicts it is essential to address the feelings of all parties. We will consider a conflict resolution model which you can use to discover the true causes of conflict within your team, and which will enable you to choose the best option to achieve a win-win solution.

In Session B we will look at some aspects of the management policies, procedures and approaches that help to create good working relationships. These are effective for 95% of the time with 95% of employees – and even more in well run organizations.

Session C concentrates on three techniques you will find useful in supporting team members, especially through times of conflict, that is, counselling, advising and supporting, and mentoring.

4.1 Objectives

When you have completed this workbook you will be better able to:

- use appropriate techniques to resolve conflict;
- manage your team to achieve positive relationships both with you and within the team, recognizing and defusing conflict in the first instance wherever practicable;
- differentiate between counselling, advising and supporting, and mentoring;
- use successful mentoring techniques.

5 Activity planner

The Work-based assignment (on page 57) will require that you spend time gathering information and talking to colleagues and people in your work team. You might like to start thinking about whom you should approach, and perhaps arrange a time to chat with them.

Session A
Managing conflict in the workplace

1 Introduction

In primitive times man dealt with conflict in one of two ways – fight or flight. It worked quite well at the time, the strongest won and everyone knew where they were. But society today is far more complex than before, and different solutions are needed. Fight and flight (at least within most societies) have been replaced by negotiation.

But what happens when negotiation fails?

This session looks at how you need to apply your management skills to dealing with conflict in the workplace. You will learn what causes conflict, what steps can be taken to handle it, and how you can make sure that everyone ends up with at least something of what they want.

2 The value of personal power

In the Super Series workbook *Building the Team* you learn about the different types of power which can enable you as a first line manager to manage your workforce. They included:

- position power – the power that comes with the job;
- expert power – acquired through being an expert in your job;
- personal power – acquired through development of personal qualities and interpersonal skills.

You may well hold all three types of power. You certainly hold position power by the very nature of your managerial role.

Activity 1

Read the comments of the two first line managers below, then decide what type/s of power they each hold.

Simon, assistant manager in a small supermarket:

'I always try to consult my staff, but in the end they do what I say because I am the boss.'

_____

James: first line manager in a tufting department of a carpet manufacturer:

'I'm not always sure what I should do in certain work situations. Even when I am reasonably sure, it's not always easy to get my team to do what I want.'

_____

We can assume that both James and Simon hold **expert power** since they would not be first line managers if they were not experts in their fields. They should also both have **position power** simply by the fact that they are managers.

Simon consults his team when he thinks it appropriate, and has enough **personal power** to be assertive when the need arises. He seems to have the balance about right.

On the other hand it looks as though James is unable to use either his position power to enforce his decisions or his personal power to get his team to buy in to them. His lack of effective influencing, persuading and negotiating skills means that he will not find it at all easy to solve any dispute that arises with his team.

So it is clear that, while it's useful to have expert power and position power as a first line manager, to be able to negotiate a resolution to a conflict situation you also need personal power.

3 Causes of conflict

Sometimes the odds on negotiations being successful are reduced, not because of the lack of skill on behalf of the negotiators, but for reasons which may be beyond their control. The main causes are as follows:

- opposing objectives;
- values being threatened;
- feedback being taken as criticism;
- situations becoming emotionally charged;
- team culture.

3.1 Opposing objectives

Sometimes you will have a person in your team who just isn't a 'team player', and who is reluctant to accept anything you say without discussion.

When you give an instruction to such a person it is important to communicate clearly and, in most situations, to explain **why** you are giving that particular instruction. Your aim is to achieve:

- a better team spirit;
- a more co-operative attitude;
- better individual performance.

However, you may also be creating a climate in which team members feel that they can query your instructions.

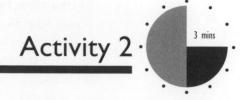

Activity 2

Having team members query your instructions has its positive side – but can also have a negative one.

What would you say could be positive about it?

_____

_____

What would you say could be negative about it?

_____

_____

Part of the positive side ought to be obvious: if people don't understand your explanations and instructions, it's good for them to feel able to ask questions. Otherwise they may make expensive mistakes.

Less obviously, perhaps, when people feel free to query instructions they are also more likely to bring problems to your attention on their own initiative.

The negative side is when individual members of the workforce get in the habit of querying the validity of your decisions rather than their own understanding of them. This can undermine your authority and can lead to arguments and bad feeling.

> A good first line manager needs to be aware of situations where confrontation is called for, skilled in the techniques of confrontation and assertive enough to use them.

Thus, while it is often a good idea to consult more experienced members of your staff, and perhaps even occasionally to encourage the whole team's participation in reaching certain decisions, you should make sure they understand that, while it's acceptable to query instructions that they don't understand, it's not acceptable for them to query your actual decisions.

You need to 'take your team with you': you can't afford to let an argument arise over every decision you make.

So how can you deal with arguments about, and objections to, your decisions?

Mina told Harriet to reorganize the job estimate files so that there was a separate file for each existing customer, with estimates for potential customers being left in the original 'general' folder. In future, each time a potential customer accepted an estimate, and thus became an 'existing customer', a new file for that customer was to be set up, and all the documentation relating to that customer was to be moved into it.

After three months Mina realized that these new files were not being set up as she had requested, and ticked Harriet off about it. Harriet was unhappy: 'It's a daft idea anyway', she said. 'It means that every time we make a sale to a new customer, I have to scroll right through the general folder to pull out all the previous estimates we've sent them even the ones they didn't accept. I haven't got time to do that every few days'.

Activity 3 · 3 mins

Describe what you would say if you were Harriet's manager.

_____

_____

_____

Harriet may well be right that the way Mina asked her to process new customer files was time-consuming, but as a manager, Mina must protect her authority: she can't simply let Harriet get away with it.

However, the answer is not simply to say: 'I'm in charge, do what I say – or else'. Harriet may obey, but she will resent this approach, and the working relationship may be seriously damaged.

Mina should:

- use her communication skills to make sure that Harriet has a full and fair opportunity to give her side of the story;
- take accurate notes.

If the problem is not resolved at this stage but becomes a disciplinary or grievance situation, accurate notes are particularly important. Mina should check the main points with Harriet to make sure that the notes record the situation correctly.

Mina might approach Harriet in the following way:

> 'You ignored my specific instructions, and that is unacceptable. When I give an instruction I expect it to be carried out. It's not up to you to decide whether to carry it out or not. If you have a problem with something I have asked you to do, say so there and then. I'm always prepared to listen to reasonable suggestions. Now, please get the new files separated out by Thursday. When you have done it, come back and see me, and then we'll discuss whether there's a better way of doing it in future.'

By handling the disagreement this way Mina protects her authority. While accepting that Harriet may have a point, she opens the way to resolving the problem in the future.

3.2 Threatened values

People will be unwilling to compromise if they feel that their values are being threatened. It is often difficult for us to explain precisely what we mean by our 'values', but usually it is things such as telling the truth, being tidy, doing what you say you will do, and so on. If negotiators are able to identify when one or other of the parties feel that their values are being threatened, they are more likely to be able to move the negotiations forward.

3.3 Criticism

A large percentage of the manager's (and negotiator's) time is spent in giving feedback. It is the only way in which other people can measure the impact of their actions.

Feedback can be seen by the person receiving it as either constructive comment or as criticism. If the latter, it is likely to result in conflict. However, if you are careful to use interpersonal skills, then any feedback you give should be received in the right way.

3.4 Roused emotions

Any situation in which emotions are aroused is going to be difficult to handle. This is where transactional analysis can be useful. By appealing to the Adult in the other person you should be able to bring the discussion onto a more neutral, impersonal level, and then explore the problem more calmly.

3.5 Team culture

Negative team culture can make negotiations extremely difficult.

> When Jean took over as first line manager in the training department of a company supplying parts to the armed forces, she found that the members of her team were all ex-military personnel with a strong dislike of taking instructions from a woman.

In such situations there is little that first line managers can do except invoke their position power and try, over time, to use their personal power to win the team over.

4 Resolving conflict situations

There are many ways of handling conflict, from taking formal disciplinary action at one extreme to deciding to ignore the situation at the other. However, as a first line manager it is in your interest to use all the skills you have learned in this workbook to negotiate an outcome that is acceptable to both sides.

You may be personally involved in the conflict or you may have to deal with conflict between two members of your workforce.

4.1 Conflict involving you personally

Jerry was sent over to the warehouse to talk to the packers about new rules for disposing of waste packing materials. The packers, who were a notoriously difficult bunch, shuffled and sniggered through Jerry's five-minute presentation. There were several interruptions to ask deliberately silly questions and Jerry's confidence was badly dented. She finished by saying 'You may think it's a joke, but you'll be laughing on the other side of your faces when Mr Khan does his next inspection'. This was greeted with derision.

Activity 4   3 mins

What was the problem in this situation? What could Jerry have done about it?

_____

_____

The packers were a team, with common values and attitudes. The problem was that their values were negative ones from Jerry's point of view. The packers' culture allowed them to break all the normal rules of politeness in order to make her life difficult. Jerry's own outburst at the end only made things worse. The episode would have damaged her authority, and her attempt to get them to buy into the new disposal procedures would probably have failed.

A team, then, starts out with a strong sense of its identity, position and values, and is capable of maintaining them in the face of outside pressure.

When you are addressing your own team, you should be able to assume that they will have a positive attitude towards you. When you are negotiating with them there should be no major barriers to overcome.

> Teams are likely to resist challenges to their accepted beliefs, attitudes and practices.

With an uncommitted or actually hostile team it is different. Even the world's greatest negotiator would have trouble winning them over in five minutes flat. You need to do some work behind the scenes in order to overcome – or at least weaken – some of the barriers.

Activity 5 ·

5 mins

Here are two approaches that Jerry could adopt towards a team with a strongly negative position. Write down what you think of each of them.

'Come on, guys, give me a break. I've had a hard day and I could do without all this aggro.'

_____

_____

'I've come to explain this new procedure to you because Mr Khan has instructed me to. So let's just get it over with, shall we?'

_____

_____

In the first version, Jerry is basically pleading with the packers to be nice to her. In the second she is invoking Mr Khan's authority – passing the buck, in other words. Both are poor approaches because they undermine Jerry's authority and weaken her ability to negotiate.

Here is a model for how Jerry could have approached her task. It is all about influencing the attitude of the packing team.

It is important for Jerry to have the packers' team leader on her side, so she should talk to him beforehand.

She could perhaps ask the team leader to introduce the briefing, thus adding extra credibility to the event. This will ensure that Jerry has at least one sympathetic listener in the audience.

Jerry should identify one of the packers to work on. This person should be an opinion former – a person who has a strong influence on the rest of the team. If this person takes a responsible and positive attitude to health and safety issues, all the better.

She should talk privately to the opinion former and find out how the team is likely to react to the new rules, and the real reasons for their opposition. If she can deal with these problems constructively, she can then ask for advice and invite practical help during the presentation. This should mean a second sympathetic listener.

The next stage is the short briefing itself. Jerry should use the connection she has already made with the team leader and the opinion former by saying things such as:

'Sam's already mentioned to me that you are concerned about. . .'

'. . .and I know Kevin agrees with me. . .'

She can also ask Sam and Kevin to explain or reinforce some points for her. This will help her to convince the team. The logic is that this team doesn't start out with any confidence in Jerry, but does have confidence in Sam and Kevin. Jerry can use this fact to win their acceptance of her message.

4.2 Conflict between other people

When you are having to resolve conflict between other people the chances of success are greatly improved if:

■ each side respects the needs and feelings of the other;
■ each side tries to understand first, then be understood;
■ neither side feels superior or more powerful;
■ each side honestly communicates their thoughts and feelings;
■ each side participates voluntarily;
■ the desired outcome for both sides is to achieve a win-win situation.

The remainder of this session looks at one approach to solving conflict between members of your staff.

5 The 4-step model for resolving conflict

Nearly all conflicts involve underlying emotional issues. The stronger the feelings, the more difficult the resolution. Therefore, to resolve a conflict, it is essential to address the feelings of each side.

The following model for resolving conflict focuses in particular on identifying and understanding emotions.

Step 1 Seek to understand

Remember to focus on the feelings behind the behaviour rather than the behaviour itself.

- Get each side to reveal their true feelings.
- Confirm that they are committed to solving the problem.
- Seek to understand the causes of each side's feelings.
- Summarize what you have understood.
- Find out what the underlying emotional needs are that are not being met.
- Check that each side has heard the other side's feelings about the conflict – and understood them.
- Show empathy.
- Ask: What would help them feel better?

Step 2 Clarify the objectives

- Decide what your main objective is in seeking a solution.

Step 3 Explore the options

- Encourage as many suggestions for solutions as possible (without evaluating them).
- Discuss each side's feelings about each option.
- Consider the implications of each option.

Step 4 Agree a solution

- Choose a final solution which optimizes positive feelings and minimizes negative feelings.

Activity 6 · 3 mins

EXTENSION 1
You might like to read chapter 4 of Roger Bennett's book *Personal Effectiveness*. It focuses on managing a team and suggests ways of handling conflict.

You are a first line manager for Creative Images Ltd, which is a medium-sized company in the advertising industry. Peter Naven and Graham Sansom are two experienced members of your work team. Unfortunately they just don't seem to be able to work together and are continually bickering and arguing. You notice that they frequently accuse each other of interfering with each other's work. In fact they are so unco-operative towards each other that their behaviour is affecting the performance of the whole team.

What is the first step you should take to deal with this situation?

_____

_____

You may have said one of the following.

■ 'Have them both in my office and talk to them about it'.
■ 'Find out what's going on.'
■ 'Try to discover what's behind the problem.'

These are all sensible answers to give. The first step is obviously to **find out the facts** and make sure they understand each other's point of view.

Activity 7

What sort of information would you want to find out from Peter and Graham?

_____

_____

_____

_____

You might have suggested the following.

■ How does each of them see the problem?
■ How long have they been working together, and when did the trouble first start?
■ Is there any personal problem between them outside work?
■ How well defined are the jobs done by Peter and Graham?

The aim at this stage is to collect all the evidence without prejudging the outcome. When you think you have gathered all the facts you can move on to the next step, **clarifying your objectives.**

Activity 8

3 mins

Tick one of the following to indicate what will be your main objective in trying to resolve the conflict between Peter and Graham.

To resolve the matter at all costs ☐

To get the team's performance back to full efficiency ☐

To get Peter and Graham to be friends ☐

To discipline them ☐

To adopt the objective of resolving the matter at all costs may meant that you have to be prepared to dismiss the two staff members. If you aim to get them to be friends, you may have set yourself an impossible task. Alternatively, deciding to discipline Peter and Graham is prejudging the issue. The most important priority for you as first line manager is achievement of the task. Your main objective, therefore, is likely to be 'To get the team's performance back to full efficiency'.

The next step is to **explore the options.**

Activity 9

3 mins

You now know certain facts relating to the problem between Peter and Graham. These are as follows.

■ They have worked together in the past.

■ The disagreements are entirely about job responsibilities and whose job it is to do what.

■ You value the technical skills and creative output of both men.

Suggest two possible solutions that will achieve your objective of getting the team's performance back to full efficiency.

_____

_____

It is important for you to keep your main objective in mind when looking at alternative solutions. You may have suggested some of the following options.

- Redefine and clarify Peter and Graham's job descriptions.
- Move one of them into another team so they don't have to work together.
- Reorganize the two jobs so that there's clearly no overlap of responsibilities.
- Confront Peter and Graham and challenge their behaviour.
- Meet with both of them. Explain the impact of their behaviour on the rest of the staff and offer to help them talk through the problem together to try to resolve any differences.

Once you have identified a number of options, the next step is to choose the best one to meet your main objective. Choosing the best option isn't always easy. The secret is to go through each course of action and work out the likely result of selecting that option.

The sorts of questions you need to ask here are as follows.

- How will this option work out?
- What will be the overall effect on the team?
- How far will this solution go towards meeting my objective?
- What are the costs (financial and otherwise) of taking this action?
- Will I be satisfied with the outcome?
- Will it solve the problem in the long term?
- What new problems might it give rise to?

Activity 10

5 mins

One of the proposed solutions to your problem was to move either Peter or Graham to another team so they don't have to work together. Now look ahead and try to work out the possible results of taking this action.

_____

_____

_____

You may have suggested some of these possible outcomes.

■ Your team may lose technical or creative skills, which can't easily be replaced.
■ You may have to retrain other staff members to fill any gaps resulting from Peter or Graham's departure.
■ Arguments may flare up again whenever the two come into contact with each other because their dispute has never been resolved.
■ The problem may be resolved.

After you have worked out the implications of all the options in the same way, you are ready to choose a solution. You need to involve both Peter and Graham in this last step because there may still be factors (feelings, other causes of conflict) that you have missed in earlier stages.

But once the solution is reached, it must be made clear that your decision is final and no further arguments will be considered.

6 Achieving a win-win situation

Activity 11 · 3 mins

Highlight the square in this matrix which should represent the best outcome of a negotiation.

	Win	Lose
Win	Win – Win	Win – Lose
Lose	Lose – Win	Lose – Lose

It may seem tempting for one side to win and the other to lose, but this often proves counter-productive because:

■ if one side has clearly 'lost the argument' it may be repudiated by more senior people on that side;
■ a losing negotiator may feel resentful, and may seek revenge at some later date.

The best outcome is where both sides perceive themselves as winning.

Naturally, a result in which **neither** side wins is an outright failure.

Self-assessment 1

12 mins

1   You can influence action on a decision most successfully by using your
    _____.

2   People will be unwilling to compromise if they feel that their _____ are being threatened.

3   The chances of resolving a conflict are greatly improved if each side respects the _____ and _____ of the other.

4   Suggest two reasons for explaining to your team **why** you are giving that particular instruction.

    _____

    _____

    _____

5   What three actions are involved in step 3 of the conflict resolution model?

    _____

    _____

    _____

Answers to these questions can be found on pages 63–4.

7 Summary

- As a first line manager you have three kinds of power:

    - position power;
    - expert power;
    - personal power.

- When disagreements arise, you should protect your power while accepting any valid points that the other person has to make.

- You should only use disciplinary procedures as a very last resort. It's far better to use persuasion and encouragement whenever possible.

- The main causes of conflict are:

    - opposing objectives;
    - values being threatened;
    - feedback being taken as criticism;
    - situations becoming emotionally charged;
    - team culture.

- The four steps in resolving conflict are:

    - seek to understand;
    - clarify the objectives;
    - explore the options;
    - agree a solution.

- You must always use your power for the good of the team and to further its defined tasks.

Session B
Managing positively

1 Introduction

In this session, we'll look at the positive aspects of leading teams to achieve a harmonious working environment. Such an environment does not come about by happy accident. It owes much to the skill and attitude of the team leader, who can make a real difference to the spirit with which a team performs and so help them to achieve the organization's standards for such key performance indicators as quality, delivery, safety, absence and staff turnover.

Team leaders work in the front line of employment relations. Signs of unhappiness, disaffection, disagreements between individuals, lack of comprehension of organizational policies and a reluctance to observe the rules and procedures that flow from them should be apparent to the team leader long before they come to the notice of senior management. Many or most problems should be resolvable at this first level, before they have had a chance to ferment into a more stubborn issue over which people may take up entrenched positions.

However, in organizations where the positive approaches described and advocated in this session are applied by team leaders, it is much less likely that managers need be concerned about the threat of employment tribunal cases, or other aspects of poor working relationships such as low morale, poor productivity, indifferent service and quality standards or, ultimately, the withdrawal of labour in unofficial or official disputes.

2 Achieving harmony at work

The dictionary defines harmony as:

> 'agreement, or concord. In music, a combination of notes which form chords of melodious sound.'

The team leader is the person who should strive to achieve this desirable condition within the team, just as the conductor of a brass band or an orchestra ensures that the sounds produced by individual players combine to produce the desired effect. Team leaders' lives are certainly much happier when an atmosphere of agreement and concord prevails.

For a conductor, there is a written score to refer to, which sets out in black and white the composer's intentions. All the players have a copy of it, can read it and are broadly committed to what the composer wishes them to do. Professional musicians have reached a defined standard of competence. This means that the conductor can be confident that all can use their instruments as required by the composer. In a military band, there is also a framework of military discipline and imposed respect for senior rank.

Activity 12

5 mins

List three factors from your own experience of work which can make a team leader's task more difficult than that of a military band leader or orchestra conductor.

_____

_____

_____

The factors which you have identified probably include:

- people who aren't competent to do the job required of them;
- individuals who are uncommitted to the company's objectives, or who don't understand them;
- rivalries between individuals who have differing ideas about how best to do the work;
- people who would simply prefer doing a different job;
- individuals who don't understand what is required of them;

- lack of respect for the team leader by one or more of the team;
- resentment by some members who believe others aren't doing their share of the work.

If a brass band suffered from some or all of these adverse factors, how harmonious do you think its overall sound would be? Discord would prevail and the composer, if listening, would hardly recognize the work.

Activity 13

3 mins

Complete the following sentences using the words provided.

SELECTION   EARN   TRAINING   EXPLAINED   FAVOURS

1   If someone isn't competent to do the job, this is probably because of poor _____ and _____.

2   An uncommitted employee often has not had the organization's policies _____ to them intelligibly.

3   Rivalries between individuals may arise when a team leader apparently _____ some team members by comparison with others.

4   A team leader must _____ the respect of all team members.

The answers can be found on page 65.

As a team leader, you have the responsibility to ensure that none of these barriers to harmonious working exists. You may need to act directly, or by influencing your manager or other specialist managers to act.

3 Selection and training

An employee unable to do the job properly will almost certainly be unhappy, and may show signs of work-related stress. Once you recognize the problems, you should arrange whatever training and coaching is necessary to bring them up to the standard required.

Induction training is very important. Team leaders have a vital role to play in making sure new employees go through the induction process. Even if this involves some temporary inconvenience, it will help you greatly in the longer term, when employees cannot say 'Nobody told me about . . .'

If you are constantly finding team members incapable of doing the job, then you need to do something to influence the way in which they are selected. Otherwise team morale will inevitably suffer and your problems will multiply.

4 Appraising performance

Some organizations carry their staff appraisal systems through to every employee. Where this happens, it gives you the opportunity for a detailed review of an individual employee's performance. You can also find out more about what the employee thinks of your performance as a team leader.

Appraisals can be an uncomfortable experience for both parties to the interview. But, provided you are trained to carry them out and everyone knows clearly that their purpose is to help improve performance and working relationships, they should be very helpful to the quest for harmonious working.

If your organization does not have such a comprehensive appraisal system, you can still try to find a little extra time to help employees with particular problems or to support those who wish to realize their full potential within the organization.

5 Communicating with the team

You have the responsibility for implementing the organization's policies with your team – just as a conductor has to make the right sounds appear from the notes written in the music.

If team members don't understand fully what is required of them, it's your job, in the first instance, to explain what they need to do – and *why*.

Ultimately, there is a job to be done and there is no point everyone working happily together if they are not delivering what is required. If the organization is being put at risk of failure there will be a corresponding threat to the team's success.

5.1 Formal briefing systems

Some organizations use formal briefing groups, or 'tool box talks', to help put the message across. You should take full advantage of such formal structures, but never treat them as a substitute for regular, day-to-day communications on key issues with all members of your team. These issues include: quality, performance targets, safety, hygiene and housekeeping.

5.2 Listening to feedback

Communication with your team needs to be a two-way process. A potent threat to harmonious working is the feeling on behalf of an individual, or section within a team, that 'nobody listens to their concerns', perhaps about safety or perceived unfairness in the way that working rotas are arranged, or holiday dates allocated.

You need to listen to your team's problems and deal immediately with the points you believe have merit. You can either do this directly, where you have sufficient authority to do so, or through colleagues or senior managers where you need help.

5.3 'Opportunist' team briefings

Where a formal briefing system isn't in place, you may be able to find 'opportunist' occasions to talk to your team as a group. This could be at the beginning of a shift, at the end of the working week, during maintenance breaks or when the computer system has crashed. However you do it – and one of the reasons you were appointed will have been your ability to use initiative – *talking* to your team together will help get them all *working* together.

Also it will help you to sense any rivalries or unhappiness that could sow the seeds of discord if you don't deal with them promptly.

6 Earning respect from the team

In all organizations, real respect has to be *earned*. Even in the military sphere, it doesn't really come from having a sergeant's stripes or a lieutenant's 'pips'.

Activity 14

5 mins

Take the following list of factors and rate them in order of importance for earning respect from your team (from 1 = most important to 10 = least important).

Factor	Your rating
Knowing the job	
Listening to what team members think	
Setting an example, for example, in timekeeping and attendance	
Being available to talk to individuals	
Sticking to what you say	
Tackling individuals' poor performance	
Encouraging people who show promise	
Helping people who have particular temporary problems and needs	
Walking the job at least once each day or shift	
Treating everyone with respect and courtesy	

This Activity is designed to make you think hard, and there is no single 'right' answer.

In practice, all ten factors are important in a team leader's endeavours to gain respect. Every factor listed begins with a verb, a 'doing word', implying the need for *action* by the leader.

The emphasis will change from time to time, but any team leader will need to *act* positively in every way to earn the respect they need.

Activity 15

Take the ten factors listed in Activity 14 and test your own leadership style candidly against them.

■ Identify any areas to which you believe that you need to give more attention.
■ Plan any actions that you need to take to address those areas, either on your own or with assistance from your own manager or others within your organization.

If it helps, imagine you work for a manager who does the *opposite* of the ten positive actions in the way that he or she manages *you*.

Areas needing attention

_____

_____

_____

Action you need to take

_____

_____

_____

7 Motivating and monitoring

There are many approaches to the motivation of individuals and teams at work. Your organization may use several of them, and you may have experience of others elsewhere.

The aims of all the well-founded approaches are to:

■ recognize and seek out the contributions of individuals;
■ encourage all team members to accept ownership of the organization's goals;
■ ensure that the task, whatever it may be, is completed consistently to the defined standards and on time.

7.1 Monitoring effectiveness

All motivational approaches need to be monitored for their effectiveness in a particular situation. Probably the simplest and most telling way to do so is to measure the outcomes from the approach being used. This is illustrated by the following case study, involving a team working in a busy despatch department.

7.2 Case study

Six months ago the despatch department of an office stationery supplier was re-organized because performance levels were unsatisfactory. The team leader's role was re-designated as 'facilitator'. The 11 members of the team (including the facilitator) were designated as an 'autonomous working group'. They now took joint responsibility for meeting all targets. The comparative measures for before and after the change are as follows:

Factor	Performance factors	
	Before Change	*After Change*
% of items delivered on time	88.9	87.6
% of items returned damaged (inadequate packaging)	3.6	3.8
Customer complaints per week (average)	17	16
Number of accidents reported per week (average for 6 month period)	0.5	0.75
Sickness absence per employee (days per month)	0.63	0.94
Overtime payment rate hours worked (average per week)	2.9	3.9
Number of employees who left (total for six months)	3	5
Number of disciplinary proceedings begun	7	1
Equipment availability (%)	87.4	95.9

The organization's main stated aims when the new system came in were:

1 to deliver to our customers on the next day in 96% of cases with less than 1% of damage due to inadequate packaging;

2 to stabilize levels of sickness absence, overtime working and staff turnover;

3 to re-establish disciplinary standards and reduce accident levels due to indiscipline.

Activity 16 ·

Study the data and then state how closely you believe each of the three stated objectives have been met by the new working system introduced to re-motivate the department.

_____

_____

_____

Provide a short written summary giving your overall assessment of the situation now (better? worse? little or no change?) and the reasons you infer may be contributing to it.

_____

_____

_____

As with most real-life situations in management, there is no 'right' answer to the questions you were asked. What is plain from the data presented is that the organization has failed in most areas, sometimes significantly, to meet its stated objectives. You will have noted that:

■ sickness absence, accident rates and overtime working have all increased sharply;

■ the number of disciplinary actions initiated has dropped sharply, which may show that no one is now prepared to take responsibility, given the poor performance levels;

- staff turnover has increased, itself usually a symptom of poor morale, possibly good employees are leaving because of the undisciplined atmosphere;
- the former team leader's job title has changed, but was any training, coaching or management support offered to help with the transition?

If the 'proof of the pudding is in the eating', then it is apparent that the switch to a self-regulating group has not worked as intended by any *objective* measure.

The remaining team members may be very happy and taking home more overtime pay, but, happy or not, they are failing to deliver the service levels required, and that could imperil their jobs and the company's future in the competitive market for office supplies, where service is everything.

One of the few things to have improved is the availability percentage for equipment; so the team is being given the tools, but failing to do the job.

7.3 Using objective measures

Not everything is measurable, but it makes sense to use objective measures wherever reasonably practicable to assess the success, or otherwise, of motivational techniques.

Once you have assessed the outcomes from the technique, as shown in the case study, you can then look at the *process* by which it was implemented to see where it is succeeding (or failing) to deliver.

Sticking with our case study, it seems apparent that insufficient preparation, training and support management was received from more senior managers to implement a system that has been used successfully in many workplaces.

Probably also, the long-term benefits to the team and its facilitator were explained insufficiently clearly. The one thing senior management *had* delivered on was improving the efficiency of the equipment provided.

The 'before change' data show clearly that there had been problems with service performance and damage, plus a high number of formal disciplinary actions (considering there are only ten employees, excluding the team leader).

Some of this implies negative attitudes and a lack of commitment to the organization and its objectives. There is no doubt that the problems needed to be faced, using a combination of the approaches already described in this session and stressing *why* there is need for change and improvement.

Until people accept that there *is* a problem, they are very unlikely to give their support to any system or technique intended to *solve* or *lessen* it.

8 Recognizing and resolving conflict situations

8.1 Eliminating the negative

An old pop song counsels listeners to 'accentuate the positive . . . that's what gets results'.

Up to this point this session has concentrated on the positive aspects of managing. However, the real world of work is not Utopian, and negative factors arise even in the best run organizations.

The same old song advises also that you should 'eliminate the negative' so we will now tackle some of the thornier problems.

8.2 The potential for conflict

The reasons for potential conflict can be many and various, and they aren't always rational.

Problems away from work

Team members may simply not get on, for reasons that have nothing to do with work. For example:

- they may support different football teams;
- they may have a dispute outside work that you know nothing about.

Losing sympathy with the organization

Individuals may become out of sympathy with the organization. Imagine someone who has:

- stopped smoking, but still works for a cigarette company;
- lost a friend or relative in a road accident, but works for a car distributor;
- become a strict vegetarian, but works for a shop selling some animal products.

EXTENSION 2
You can find out more about how to handle bullying from ACAS.

Bullying and harassment

What begins as a bit of harmless teasing can escalate into bullying, with serious implications if it is not tackled early.

Likewise, sexual, racial or religious harassment may begin as what the instigator regards as 'harmless fun'. The victim may be thought of as 'thin skinned' or 'lacking a sense of humour'.

Custom and practice

Years ago, people often underwent initiation rites when completing an apprenticeship. Nowadays, many of these would be frowned upon and, if imposed against the victim's will, could lead to an Employment Tribunal.

Such initiation rites may be long-established custom and practice in a place of work, and can be a potential source of conflict.

Other possible examples include workplaces where it has been the practice for years to watch adult films in the relaxation area. A new employee may find this objectionable or even threatening.

Similarly, established employees may have broken many safety rules in order to finish early on Friday afternoons. Perhaps the previous team leader turned a blind eye, so when you tackle the issue, conflict could ensue.

Such sub-cultures can, if unchecked, eventually completely usurp your authority as a manager.

8.3 The team leader as 'intelligence officer'

Any of these situations – and you may think of many others – could cause conflict. It could arise either within your team, or between a member of the team and yourself as the representative of management policies and objectives.

If you are 'walking the job' regularly and talking to everyone in your team daily, or more often, you will soon start to feel the bad vibrations that emanate from various situations.

Activity 17

5 mins

Look at the following signals given by members of a team, and write down what action you would take as their team leader. Then add up to three further signals from your own experience and say what you *actually* did.

Signal 1:

Hassan and Victor always make a point of sitting a long way apart in the tea room. They have been seen to 'jostle' each other when clocking in.

Action:

_____

_____

_____

Signal 2:

Four new employees have all left one section within a few days of starting work. According to the section 'old hands' they didn't seem to fit in.

Action:

_____

_____

_____

Signal 3:

Graffiti derogatory to an ethnic group has begun to appear in the washroom. No one will admit responsibility.

Action:

_____

_____

_____

Signal 4:
A new employee has asked for a 'sub' against her wages and is very vague about why she needs it.

Action:

_____

_____

_____

Signal 5:

_____

Action:

_____

_____

_____

Signal 6:

_____

Action:

_____

_____

_____

Signal 7:

_____

Action:

_____

_____

_____

You may have made suggestions along the following lines.

1   Talk to Hassan and Victor individually. Get them to open up by using open questions beginning with 'How', 'What', 'Where', 'When', 'Why' and 'Who'. For example, you could say 'How do you think Victor is settling in to the team?' 'What does Hassan think of the new quality procedures?' Once you have a reasonable idea of what the bad feeling is about, you can try to resolve the cause. If it is a work-related problem (such as working rotas), you may be able to resolve it yourself. If not, you can try to help them see that prejudices or disputes outside work cannot be allowed to affect your team's morale and performance.

2   Question the 'old hands' as to why and how the four newcomers didn't fit in. Look for any evidence of a sub-culture – card schools, working practices outside the rules, prejudices to do with working with particular groups. If they are freezing the newcomers out, you will need to take positive steps to restore standards throughout your team.

3   Gather any evidence available from the cleaning staff and other departments. Talk to your team members individually and as a group, making it plain that this is unacceptable behaviour – whoever is doing it – and that it could represent serious misconduct. Try to discover what is at the root of it (it may be nothing directly to do with race), and if necessary encourage members to discuss the underlying issues with you, explaining that only then can you try to resolve them.

4   Ask the employee tactfully why she needs the sub, explaining that if it is for purely personal reasons it can be dealt with under the organization's normal rules. However, if someone is demanding money from her, as a sort of commission or entry fee, that could be gross misconduct and might land the person in serious trouble if they persist in the demand. If the problem persists you could encourage her to use the confidential grievance procedure, and you may eventually need assistance from your manager.

The last three signals, which you have described from your own experience, should have illustrated the benefits of constantly monitoring what goes on in your team, and taking immediate action to deal with any problems that arise.

9 Resolving conflict

In some cases, you may need help to resolve conflict situations. However, if you attune yourself to *recognizing* the signals of conflict and becoming a figure of trust for your team members, many of the situations may resolve themselves before you need additional help.

9.1 Somebody must pay ... or must they?

It is often said that we now live in a blame culture, with lawyers eager to find any offences which may result in substantial compensation for the victim and sizeable fees for them.

Whether or not that is true for society at large, you should *not* encourage such a culture to develop within your team.

Just as the best and chief reason for investigating accidents is to prevent them happening again, so the chief reason for resolving conflict should be to achieve more harmonious working relationships and a generally more pleasant, positive atmosphere in which to work. Fear of being blamed or disciplined unjustly will make it much harder to reach the root of any problem, which is no good to anyone.

You need to be seen as:

■ a leader who can be trusted to act, first and foremost, in the interests of fairness and improved working relationships for the future;
■ someone committed to resolving the problem, wherever possible, to the satisfaction of all parties *without* seeking to apportion blame as though in a court of law.

9.2 The ideal 'win–win' situation ...

Most of the time, your aim should be to achieve a settlement that allows all parties to believe that they have achieved something from the negotiation. For example, it might be possible to encourage some give and take over issues such as working rotas, overtime allocation, tea breaks or out-of-hours parking spaces in order to achieve the desirable 'win–win' outcome.

9.3 ... and the realities of the law

However, there can be no compromise over some issues, including those where safety or other working practices are concerned that conflict with the law.

An organization cannot condone practices that are illegal, and you can have no authority to do so on its behalf.

If another employee's safety or employment rights were to be compromised by your complicity, then the matter could end up being resolved by an Employment Tribunal, with inevitable negative results for the organization and for you.

10 Grievance procedures

These procedures can have a beneficial part to play in resolving potential conflicts of many kinds.

Activity 18

3 mins

Give three or four examples of grievances that employees might wish to raise. One example you might think of is being bullied by other employees.

_____

_____

_____

_____

There could be many items on your list, including:

- being passed over continually for promotion;
- never being offered overtime (*or* required to do too much overtime);
- sexual or racial harassment;
- being given all the 'rotten work', for example, piece work with limited earnings potential;
- being required to do work offensive to religious beliefs;
- being ignored by colleagues ('sent to Coventry') for working too hard.

There can be no definitive list for grievances, and one person will shrug off something that another will regard as a major problem.

It is unlikely that every aggrieved employee will be satisfied with the solution available through following the formal grievance procedures.

Some grievances may be more imaginary than real, while others may be impossible to resolve without changing the entire organization, which is probably impractical.

Even so, having an official channel for grievances may be a useful safety valve to those involved.

10.1 Positive use of grievance procedure

The very existence of a grievance procedure encourages people to use it, provided that there is evidence that the organization takes it seriously. Some problems are solvable, given goodwill and trust.

It is far better for employees to feel that they can do something, rather than 'nursing' their grievance and perhaps eventually leaving the organization and claiming constructive dismissal before an Employment Tribunal. If a Tribunal hearing arises, having and following a formal, recorded grievance procedure shows that your organization has tried to help employees to resolve their problems within its own structure and the law.

10.2 Role of the first line manager and team leader

First line managers and team leaders are the most likely first point of contact, and should be the people best able to resolve problems quickly. You need to show staff that you will try to resolve their genuine concerns without delay.

As with many aspects of management, grievance handling is more art than science. The approaches advocated in this session, used conscientiously, will help you to:

■ keep the number of perceived grievances raised to a minimum;
■ deal sympathetically and objectively with those that reach you;
■ prevent many or most of them escalating into a crisis that diverts attention from the main objectives agreed for your team.

Self-assessment 2

1 Name four actions that a team leader can take to help earn the respect and trust of the team.

_____

_____

_____

_____

2 The use of team briefing will ensure that everyone in the team knows _____ is required of them and that everyone gets the _____ message.

3 Team leaders need to be good _____ and able to _____ on what they hear when necessary.

4 Team leaders should ensure that all new team members go through an _____ process when they first join the organization.

5 Assigning _____ to one party or another is always _____ in resolving conflict situations.

6 Give three examples of an individual employee's concerns which a well-founded grievance procedure might help resolve.

_____

_____

_____

_____

7 Custom and practice may be evidence of sub-cultures which, if not addressed, can _____ your authority as a leader.

8 Name one potential benefit from using a formal appraisal system;

■ for the appraiser;
■ for the person being appraised.

For the appraiser:

_____

For the person being appraised:

_____

Answers to these questions will be found on pages 64–5.

11 Summary

■ Harmony is the desirable condition where people work together cheerfully and give of their best to help you achieve organizational objectives.

■ First line managers can make a major contribution to achieving good working relationships.

■ The selection, induction, initial and continuing training of staff are vital aspects of developing both individual and team performance and high morale.

■ Briefing, formal or informal, is a powerful tool that you can use to ensure that all team members know what is required of them and get the same message.

■ Communication is a two way process – team leaders need to listen attentively and take note of what they hear.

■ Respect will be earned by treating people with respect and courtesy and applying appropriate management techniques.

■ It is essential to monitor the effectiveness of motivational approaches and make adjustments to suit the organizational circumstances.

■ First line managers should recognize actual and potential conflict situations and resolve them wherever possible.

■ Attributing blame is as unhelpful in conflict situations as it is when investigating accidents. The object in both areas should be to prevent recurrence of the problem.

■ Grievance procedures, properly used and respected, can be a positive force for resolving situations that could lead to conflict.

■ While the law is always there in the background of all employment practices, managing positively will keep you in step with it and keep you away from potentially disastrous Employment Tribunal hearings.

Session C
Counselling and mentoring

1 Introduction

So far in this workbook we have looked at the causes of conflict, how you can try to avoid it occurring and the things that you can do to resolve conflict if it does occur. In this final session we will examine some of the strategies you can use to support team members who have experienced conflict at work and need to be helped to overcome some of the consequences of it.

2 Five ways to support your team members

You can support the members of your team in a variety of ways, including training, coaching, counselling, advising and supporting, and mentoring. It can all seem very confusing to the layperson and many people would find it difficult to explain the difference between them.

Activity 19

6 mins

See if you can write down your own definition of each of the following terms in the spaces below.

Training

_____

_____

Coaching

_____

_____

Counselling

_____

_____

Advising and supporting

_____

_____

Mentoring

_____

_____

_____

If your definitions are similar to the ones below you are on the right lines.

Training is a planned and structured process aimed at improving people's work-related skills and knowledge.

Coaching is an ongoing, one-to-one process in which a team leader works with members of the team to solve problems linked to the team members' work, the purpose being to enable them to develop further skills and competencies.

Counselling is again a one-to-one activity, but this time it is not necessarily related to work. The aim is for the counsellor to assist the counsellees to help themselves to solve a problem that affects them personally. People being counselled are helped to:

- explore their personal feelings, thoughts and actions;
- reach a better understanding of themselves and how they fit into their environment;
- make appropriate decisions or take relevant action to solve a personal problem.

Advising and **supporting** in the workplace environment generally involve giving practical help when a problem arises. For example, if members of your team are made redundant there are many ways in which you could help to prepare them for such an upheaval – such as researching the availability of retraining programmes, or locating vacancies in other areas of the organization.

Mentoring can be defined as facilitating someone else's career development. The mentor becomes a trusted adviser and guide to the learner and takes him or her under their wing. Mentoring has been used for many years, for example in the old apprentice system when master craftsmen kept a fatherly eye on the young apprentices working with them. Very often it is something that evolves informally through a personal relationship between a young member of the team and an older, more experienced member. The benefits can be so great that in recent years many organizations have set up more formal mentoring arrangements.

The remainder of this session looks in detail at two of these support roles, counselling and mentoring.

3 Counselling

As a first line manager, you probably spend much of your time telling people what to do. But in counselling, the approach is different. Your role is to give support to your team members while they themselves come to terms with, or solve, a problem of their own.

Frequently the problem manifests itself in relation to the team member's work situation, but there can be other, hidden causes, often personal in nature, which need to be identified and dealt with. For example, someone whose concentration at work has deteriorated may discover that, although the most obvious cause is poor sleep, the underlying cause is to do with poor family relationships or depression.

Activity 20

Why is it better for people to find their own solutions to their problems rather than being told by someone else what to do?

_____

_____

You may have said that people are much more likely to adopt a solution if they have arrived at it themselves.

This section describes the basics of counselling. However, a word of warning – it is a role which carries a great deal of responsibility because the counsellor is in such a position of trust, and for this reason it is often a role taken by more senior people in an organization. So it might be a good idea to treat the information given here simply as an introduction to the skill of counselling. Many excellent books and courses are available if you want to go into the subject in more depth.

3.1 The counselling process

Counselling is a one-to-one conversation between a counsellor and counsellee. It has three stages:

1 Exploration of the problem.
2 Understanding (by both parties) of the causes.
3 Commitment to action.

3.2 Exploring the problem

The first stage is to explore the problem from the counsellees' point of view. They should be doing ninety per cent of the talking.

To encourage this you need to develop skills in:

■ showing attention;
■ asking open questions;
■ active listening (by paraphrasing what the counsellees have said and summarizing at regular intervals);

- getting the counsellees to progress from making generalizations to expressing their specific feelings and thoughts about the problem;
- moving towards the future (getting the counsellees to think about how they would like things to be).

It is useful to look a bit more closely at the first two of these skills.

A good counsellor shows **attention** by giving verbal and non-verbal signs to encourage the speaker.

Activity 21

12 mins

In the space below list as many signs as you can think of that would indicate that you are paying attention. You may find it helpful to think about someone you have talked to recently who seemed to be listening and someone whose attention seemed to be elsewhere. What was the difference between them?

_____

_____

_____

_____

You could have suggested that the good listener used eye contact, smiled and nodded, inclined their head and body towards you, used open gestures (that is, they didn't cross their arms in front of them), made encouraging noises such as 'ah-ah', and mirrored your own body language to show empathy. For more information on the use of body language see *Communication Process* in this series.

The second important skill is to **ask questions** in the right way. Questions should be **open**, that is, they should encourage the counsellee to talk, rather than just answering 'yes' or 'no'. This means that you must avoid being judgemental, or telling the counsellee what to do.

For a detailed discussion of listening and questioning skills see *Communication Process* in this series.

3.3 Understanding the causes

You can use various techniques to help counsellees to understand the causes of their problems. These include the following.

Offering alternative frames of reference

Encourage the counsellees to see the problem in a new light. They might find that they themselves could change so that they can cope with the situation better.

Self disclosure

If you think it appropriate, make the counsellees more relaxed by indicating that you have experienced similar problems or feelings yourself. However, there is a danger here that they could feel that the focus has moved away from their own feelings.

Confrontation

Very gently challenge what they are saying. You could say, for example 'Come on, do you really think that you have no friends in the team?' This may help them to explore alternative ways of perceiving the problem.

Remember, your approach should always be supportive and aimed at letting the counsellees explore the problem for themselves.

Activity 22

You are counselling Ruth. She is in tears because you have recently had to tell her that her work is not up to scratch. During the counselling session it appears that her husband was made redundant three months ago and he is showing no signs of looking for another job. He is also becoming moody and says that she is picking on him.

Which of the following responses would be the best for you to choose?

a 'Try to forget about it. After all it's his problem. Your priority is to look after your own job and that's not going too well at the moment.'

b 'What makes you think that he isn't trying to find another job?'

c 'I suppose you are afraid that he will eventually give up all idea of working again.'

d 'If I were you I would threaten to stop supporting him unless he starts trying to find another job.'

The best response would be b. You are encouraging Ruth to explore the situation and make sure she understands it fully before doing anything drastic. Response a doesn't help her to look at the problem at all, while in response c you are making assumptions about how she feels. In d you are telling her what she should do without giving her the opportunity to make her own decision.

3.4 Commitment to action

In this final stage of the counselling process your task is to help counsellees come to a positive conclusion about how to tackle the problem. You need to encourage them to:

- clarify any action that they have decided they should take;
- express it in terms of concrete, obtainable goals;
- identify the relevant strengths and resources they already have;
- identify the skills and resources they still need.

3.5 After the counselling session

It might take several counselling sessions before counsellees reach the final stage of commitment to action. Once they get there, you should end the session by agreeing an action plan and setting a review date. By now they should be feeling that, while they may not have found the perfect solution, at least they can now see the situation clearly and have found a positive way forward.

You should also make it clear that you will always be available for further sessions. This ongoing moral support will encourage the counsellees to explore their own problems and find solutions more effectively in the future.

4 Professional help

In certain counselling situations you will find that counsellees' problems are too complex to be solved in a normal counselling session. For example, during the exploration stage it may become apparent that the counsellee would benefit from more specialized help.

Many local support services are available, many of them free. They include:

■ local authority and government information services;
■ professional stress counsellors (private or provided by the NHS);
■ local solicitors who participate in the Law Society's free advice scheme.

Many national organizations offer free help. The problem areas they cover include:

■ alcohol;
■ emotional support;
■ money and debt;
■ disability;
■ drugs.

Activity 23

12 mins

Obtain a copy of *Yellow Pages* and find the section on Helplines at the beginning of the book.

Note down the name of an organization that offers advice and support in each of the following categories.

Alcohol

_____

Emotional support

_____

Money and debt

_____

Disability

_____

Drugs

_____

You could have found many organizations that specialize in each category, including Alcoholics Anonymous (alcohol), Relate and Samaritans (emotional support), the Consumer Credit Counselling Service (money and debt), DIAL UK (disability), and the National Drugs Helpline (drugs).

5 Mentoring

EXTENSION 3
For more on mentoring, see _One-to-one Training and Coaching Skills_ by Roger Buckley and Jim Caple.

At the beginning of this session we learned that mentoring involves experienced people acting as guides and confidant(e)s to less experienced colleagues, with the aim of helping them to gain skills and develop their careers.

5.1 Who should act as a mentor?

Unlike a coach, a mentor should not be directly involved in the learner's work, so it is not a role that the immediate line manager should take on. This is because mentoring should be seen as a partnership, and this does not sit comfortably with the manager/subordinate relationship.

Often it will be the learner who chooses the mentor rather than the other way round and the relationship may last for a set period of time, say six months.

Typically a mentor will be a colleague or more experienced friend of the learner, who is not necessarily a subject expert, but who is able to give moral and practical support in the process of career development.

5.2 The mentoring cycle

There are four stages in the mentoring cycle. They are:

■ identifying needs and setting objectives;
■ organizing the mentees' development;
■ monitoring progress;
■ reviewing the objectives if necessary.

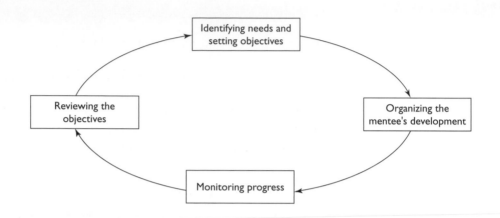

Identifying needs and setting objectives

It is vital to carry out some initial needs assessment. You can achieve this by discussing with the mentees what skills they have at present and the skills they need to develop.

Organizing the mentees' development

Your most important task is to **motivate** the mentees to take on the responsibility for their own development. You can also help by:

■ coaching;
■ counselling;
■ organizing special projects;
■ making use of your contacts and networks.

Activity 24

Think about people at work for whom you could act as mentor. What special project could you help them to organize that would encourage them to develop? Which of your contacts could you use to help the project be successful?

_____

_____

_____

Whatever project you have chosen, you must be confident that the mentees have the ability to complete the project successfully, and that you very clearly define what the objectives of the project are.

Monitoring progress

It is essential that the mentees are clear about the progress they are making. They need to know where they have been successful and where they still need to develop.

Revisiting the objectives

You will need to do this if the monitoring process shows that the current objectives will not meet the mentees' identified learning needs.

The main thing to remember in regard to the mentoring cycle as a whole is that mentoring is a constantly evolving process, with each stage of the cycle being dependent on the previous stage while at the same time feeding into the next stage.

5.3 The mentor's role

The mentor's main role is to:

■ discuss work-related problems and help the mentee to find solutions;
■ where appropriate, talk through the mentee's work and give informal feedback;
■ introduce the mentee to new ideas or people in the organization who can be helpful;
■ provide guidance based on his or her greater experience of the organization's way of doing things;
■ give moral support to boost the mentee's confidence.

Activity 25

Thinking about your own team members, can you identify one or more people who would benefit from having a mentor? If so, have a word with them to see how they feel about it and ask them if they can suggest someone whom they feel would be a good mentor for them.

Then explain to the potential mentor what the role entails and let them take it from there.

6 Confidentiality

Whatever your role in regard to your team members – whether you are acting as coach, counsellor, adviser or mentor – remember that whatever is said between you is completely confidential. You should never involve third parties without consulting the team members first.

Self-assessment 3

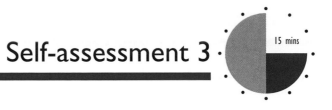

15 mins

1 What is the key difference between counselling and mentoring?

2 What three steps are involved in counselling?

3 What is the purpose of open questions?

4 What is the only situation in which you can tell a third party what has been discussed in a counselling or mentoring session?

Answers to these questions can be found on page 65.

7 Summary

- There are a number of ways to support your team members, including training, coaching, counselling, advising and supporting, and mentoring.

- Training is a planned and structured process aimed at improving people's work-related skills and knowledge.

- Coaching is an ongoing, one-to-one process in which a line manager works with a member of the team to solve problems linked to the team member's work.

- Counselling involves one person assisting another to help himself or herself to explore personal feelings, reach a better understanding of themselves, and make appropriate decisions to solve personal problems.

- Advising and supporting in the workplace environment generally involve giving practical help when a problem arises.

- Mentoring involves a trusted adviser and guide facilitating someone else's career development.

- Many professional organizations offer free help to people with personal or financial problems. One way to contact them is through *Yellow Pages*.

- Confidentiality is an essential component of all support activities.

Performance checks

▪ 1 Quick quiz

Question 1   The chances of success are greatly improved if each side honestly communicates their _____ and _____ .

Question 2   Give two reasons why it is not a good idea for one side to win a dispute outright and the other to lose.

_____

_____

Question 3   What do you understand by 'custom and practice', and how can it affect working relationships?

_____

_____

Question 4   Why is it important to avoid assigning blame to one party or another when trying to resolve problems within your team?

_____

_____

Question 5   What do you understand by achieving a 'win–win' situation following a dispute? Are there circumstances where it is not an 'achievable outcome'?

_____

_____

Question 6   Apart from training, what are the **four** ways in which you can support members of your team?

_____

_____

Question 7   Name **three** techniques that you can use to help counsellees to understand the causes of their problems.

_____

_____

_____

Question 8   Why shouldn't line managers take on a mentoring role in relation to one of their team members?

_____

_____

Answers to these questions can be found on page 66.

2 Workbook assessment

60 mins

Trouble had been brewing for some time. It started when Jaimie had been slow getting some work done, and it meant that everyone else had fallen behind. Because of this, the team had failed to hit their targets that week and missed out on the chance for a bonus. Gradually, relationships between Jaimie and two other team members had deteriorated. It often took some small incident for them to start arguing and once or twice it had got quite heated. Before long it was clear that the situation would explode and there could be a major problem.

Unfortunately, Jaimie tended to be a bit slow. He was good at what he did, but very thorough, and sometimes did unnecessary work to complete tasks that were perfectly OK already. The others tended to regard him as a bit of a fusspot, but when something special needed doing, Jaimie was the one who did it, because he was such a perfectionist.

As the leader of the team:

1   How would you deal with this conflict in the team?
2   What steps could you take to support Jaimie to prevent the problem re-occurring?

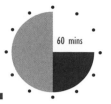

3 Work-based assignment

S/NVQ
B6

The time guide for this assignment gives you an idea of how long it is likely to take you to write up your findings. You will find that you need to spend some additional time gathering information, perhaps talking to colleagues and thinking about the assignment.

Your response to this assignment may form useful evidence for your S/NVQ portfolio. The assignment is designed to help you demonstrate:

- your ability to act assertively;
- your ability to communicate;
- your ability to manage yourself;
- your ability to influence others.

What you should do

Think of a particularly difficult dispute that you have had to deal with at work in the past. It should involve a situation that caused problems between members of your staff.

Describe the specific nature of the conflict, its causes and the individuals involved. There may be documents that you can refer to which will give a background to the problem.

You may also need to interview the staff members involved to get their reaction to how you handled the situation. This may be sensitive, so you will need to use your judgement as to whether interviews are appropriate.

Then answer the following questions about the way you resolved the conflict.

- What impact did it have on the team and their ability to complete their team objectives?
- To what extent did you use your personal rather than position power when negotiating a resolution?
- Did you encounter any specific difficulties in dealing with people that you felt inadequate to deal with?
- Did you use the 4-step model for resolving conflict in this situation? If so, give details and describe how successful it was.
- How did you ensure that the parties to the dispute were satisfied with your decision?

You should record your findings, and then try to decide what you can deduce from the information you have collected. Your overall aim in this assignment is to answer the following questions.

- What have I discovered about how successful my negotiating was in this situation?
- Did I fully involve the parties to the dispute? How do they feel about my performance and the way I used my authority?
- How will this knowledge lead me to manage my team more effectively in the future?

What you should write

Present your findings in a structured way using appropriate sub-headings.

Add to your findings a list of key pointers that are relevant to your future negotiating activities.

Reflect and review

■ 1 Reflect and review

Now that you have completed your work on managing conflict in the workplace, let's review the workbook objectives. The first objective was:

■ use appropriate techniques to resolve conflict

There are many reasons why conflict might result in disruption in the workplace. This is very often caused by poor communication. It is the first line manager's responsibility to identify sources of conflict and use the skills of persuasion and negotiation to get each party to agree to a compromise. You may want to think about the following points.

■ How is conflict currently dealt with in my work team?

_____

_____

_____

■ In future, how will I make myself aware of conflict situations when they arise, and how will I ensure that it is resolved in a win–win way?

_____

_____

_____

The second objective was:

■ manage your team to achieve positive relationships both with you and within the team, recognizing and defusing conflict in the first instance wherever practicable.

First line managers work at the interface between management policies and procedures and employees. They are in the best position to influence employees and create harmonious working relationships by managing their team with respect, applying well established approaches to motivation and communications, and comparing the results obtained with agreed standards of performance.

■ Do you believe that you have sufficient knowledge of the approaches you should be using?

_____

■ Do you make effective use of them, or are there areas in which you should be doing more and, if so, what additional actions do you plan to take?

_____

_____

■ differentiate between counselling, advising and supporting, and mentoring

It is often thought that training and coaching are the only things that people need to aid their career development. But the best organizations offer much more in the way of support in the learning process. You may want to think more about this by asking:

■ What facilities are available to my work team in regard to counselling, advising and supporting, and mentoring?

_____

_____

_____

■ What proposals might I put to my manager to provide further support?

_____

_____

_____

■ use successful mentoring techniques

A mentoring relationship often develops informally as the result of a friendship that has been established in the workplace. But some organizations, seeing the benefits that mentoring can bring, have introduced formal systems where experienced members of the workforce are allocated as mentors to new recruits. It might be useful to think about:

■ How could I introduce a mentoring system into my workplace, and whose help would I need to do so?

_____

_____

_____

■ How could you personally benefit from being mentored by a colleague?

_____

_____

_____

2 Action plan

Use this plan to further develop for yourself a course of action you want to take. Make a note in the left-hand column of the issues or problems you want to tackle, then decide what you intend to do and make a note in column 2.

The resources you need might include time, materials, information, or money. You may need to negotiate for some of them, but they could be something easily acquired, like half an hour of somebody's time, or a chapter of a book. Put whatever you need in column 3. No plan means anything without a timescale, so put a realistic target completion date in column 4.

Finally, describe the outcome you want to achieve as a result of this plan, whether it is your own benefit or advancement, or a more efficient way of doing things.

Desired outcomes			
1 Issues	2 Action	3 Resources	4 Target completion
Actual outcomes			

3 Extensions

Extension 1	Book	*Personal Effectiveness*
	Author	Roger Bennett
	Edition	1994
	Publisher	Kogan Page
Extension 2	Book	*Bullying and Harassment at Work: A Guide for Managers and Employers*
	Edition	2006
	Publisher	ACAS (http://www.acas.org.uk and follow link to Publications)
Extension 3	Book	*One-to-one Training and Coaching Skills*
	Authors	Roger Buckley and Jim Caple
	Publisher	Kogan Page
	Edition	1996 (second edition)

4 Answers to self-assessment questions

Self-assessment 1 on page 16

1 You can influence action on a decision most successfully by using your **PERSONAL POWER**.

2 People will be unwilling to compromise if they feel that their **VALUES** are being threatened.

3 The chances of resolving a conflict are greatly improved if each side respects the **NEEDS** and **FEELINGS** of the other.

4 Reasons for explaining to you team **why** you are giving that particular instruction are that it will result in:

■ a better team spirit;
■ a more co-operative attitude;
■ better individual performance.

5 The three actions involved in step 3 of the conflict resolution model are:

- encourage as many suggestions for solutions as possible;
- discuss each side's feelings about each option;
- consider the implications of each option.

Self-assessment 2 on pages 37–8

1 Actions that a team leader can take to help earn the respect and trust of the team include:

- knowing the job;
- listening to what team members think;
- setting an example, such as good timekeeping and attendance;
- being available to talk to individuals;
- sticking to what you say;
- tackling individuals' poor performance;
- encouraging people who show promise;
- helping people who have particular temporary problems and needs;
- walking the job at least once each day or shift;
- treating everyone with respect and courtesy.

2 The use of team briefing will ensure that everyone in the team knows **what** is required of them and that everyone gets the **same** message.

3 Team leaders need to be good **listeners** and able to **act** on what they hear when necessary.

4 Team leaders should ensure that all new team members go through an **induction** process when they first join the organization.

5 Assigning **blame** to one party or another is always **unhelpful** in resolving conflict situations.

6 Examples of an individual employee's concerns which a well founded grievance procedure might help resolve include:

- harassment or bullying;
- being passed over for promotion;
- working rotas, holiday arrangements.

7 Custom and practice may be evidence of sub-cultures which, if not addressed, can **undermine** your authority as a leader.

8 Potential benefits to appraisers from using a formal appraisal system are the chance to discuss issues in greater depth and to receive feedback from the 'appraisee' on performance as a team leader.

Potential benefits for the person being appraised are objective feedback on performance and the opportunity to raise issues and concerns in private situation.

Self-assessment 3 on page 53

1 Counselling is a one-to-one activity in which counsellees are helped to explore their personal feelings, reach a better understanding of themselves, and make appropriate decisions to solve personal problems.

Mentoring occurs when an experienced colleague becomes a trusted adviser and guide to another person in order to facilitate that person's career development.

2 Counselling involves: exploring the problem, understanding the causes, and commitment to action.

3 Open questions are designed to encourage the person who is being questioned to talk freely about the topic under discussion.

4 The only time you can involve a third party is when the counsellee has given permission for you to do so.

▌▶ 5 Answers to activities

Activity 13 on page 21

1 If someone isn't competent to do the job, this is probably because of poor SELECTION and TRAINING.

2 An uncommitted employee often has not had the organization's policies EXPLAINED to them intelligibly.

3 Rivalries between individuals may arise when a team leader apparently FAVOURS some team members by comparison with others.

4 A team leader must EARN the respect of all team members.

6 Answers to the quick quiz

Answer 1   The chances of success are greatly improved if each side honestly communicates their **THOUGHTS** and **FEELINGS**.

Answer 2   It is not a good idea for one side to win a dispute outright and the other to lose because:

- if one side has clearly lost the agreement it may be repudiated by more senior people on that side;
- a losing negotiator may feel resentful, and may seek revenge at some later date.

Answer 3   'Custom and practice' is a general term which covers unofficial working methods that have built up over time and that may be at odds with the organization's official policies. If deep rooted, such working methods can make it hard for a manager to apply the proper procedures, even if the law requires it.

Answer 4   Assigning blame to one party or another will tend to make everyone wary of the process and reluctant to get involved in it.

Answer 5   A 'win–win' situation is an outcome from a dispute such that all the parties feel that they have achieved something positive from the process, even if they didn't get *everything* they hoped for. Circumstances where this is not an achievable outcome would include any where to concede something to a party would break the law; for instance, by condoning unsafe practices, or allowing an employee to refuse to work with someone because they were of another race, sex or religion.

Answer 6   You can support members of your team by:

- coaching;
- counselling;
- advising and supporting;
- mentoring.

Answer 7   Three techniques that you can use to help counsellees to understand the causes of their problem are:

- offering alternative frames of reference;
- self disclosure;
- confrontation.

Answer 8   Line managers shouldn't take on a mentoring role in relation to one of their team members because mentoring is a partnership and doesn't sit comfortably with the manager/subordinate relationship.

7 Certificate

Completion of this certificate by an authorized person shows that you have worked through all the parts of this workbook and satisfactorily completed the assessments. The certificate provides a record of what you have done that may be used for exemptions or as evidence of prior learning against other nationally certificated qualifications.

superseries

Managing Conflict in the Workplace

....

has satisfactorily completed this workbook

Name of signatory ....

Position ....

Signature ....

Date ....

Official stamp

Pergamon
Flexible
Learning

Fifth Edition

superseries

FIFTH EDITION

Workbooks in the series:

For prices and availability please telephone our order helpline
or email

+44 (0) 1865 474010
directorders@elsevier.com